Original title:
The Snowball Fight Chronicles

Copyright © 2024 Creative Arts Management OÜ
All rights reserved.

Author: Robert Ashford
ISBN HARDBACK: 978-9916-94-310-6
ISBN PAPERBACK: 978-9916-94-311-3

Glacial Tactics

In the park where brave hearts clash,
Snowballs fly in a frosty flash.
Laughter echoes, winter's cheer,
As we hurl our icy spheres near.

Cunning plans and sneaky dives,
Behind the trees, how laughter thrives.
A snow-covered fortress stands so tall,
Yet one brave soul makes a great fall!

With stealthy moves, a crafty sneak,
Hitting your friend brings a joyful shriek.
Unexpected hits lead to surprise,
And snow-covered giggles light up our eyes.

The wintry air is filled with glee,
As snowflakes dance, wild and free.
Bald heads shine with a snowy cap,
In this hilarious snowy trap!

Blizzard Brawlers

In a world of white, the brawlers meet,
Each one armed with icy treat.
Tightly packed, their ammo is ready,
With laughter bubbling, spirits are heady.

Fury flares with every throw,
Giggles erupt, 'Oh no, oh no!'
Dodging, diving, the snowflakes swirl,
As victory dances in each twirling girl.

The ground is slick, a perilous play,
Slipping, sliding, come what may.
But with each tumble and fall we find,
The best of friends, we leave fears behind.

In snowball war, the best will grin,
For laughter's the prize, let the fun begin!
A battle of joy under skies so blue,
Where every throw turns a frown to a 'woo-hoo!'

Playful Chaos on Icy Terrain

In the glimmering fields of white,
Laughter echoes, pure delight.
Snowballs whizzing, faces bright,
Winter's joy takes off in flight.

Giant mounds of fluff arise,
Targets lurk with crafty eyes.
Dodge or throw, the cold surprise,
Friendly foes, no magic lies.

Slips and trips and bursts of cheer,
A snowman's head is rolling near.
Hot cocoa waits to soothe each tier,
Victory claimed with frozen gear.

As day turns to a chilling night,
The laughter fades, but spirits light.
A snowy truce, the end in sight,
Until next time, oh, what a sight!

Snowball Strategies of Winter

In stealthy shadows, plans are laid,
Snowballs prepped, no chance to fade.
Whispers turn to joyful trade,
Every flake a renegade.

Behind the trees, a quiet shout,
Who's the best? Let's have a rout!
Rolling balls without a doubt,
Laughs explode as they flit about.

Tactics shift with every throw,
Shivers felt from head to toe.
A sudden hit, a silly glow,
Foes unite in friendly woe.

As the sun begins to sink,
We gather 'round, our eyes all wink.
Joyful cheers and lips that clink,
In winter's chill, we find the link!

Yonder Lies the Frosty Front

On frosty fields, the ice does gleam,
A snowball launched, it sails like a dream.
Dodges aimed, and shouts that beam,
A winter's contest, pure as cream.

The snowflakes swirl, a flurry dance,
Every player takes their chance.
A hit, a splash, a circus prance,
Oh, what joy in this snowy expanse!

Strategic moves, a playful reck,
Allies form with a cheeky peck.
With icy gloves, we seal the trek,
Hurling snowballs in every check.

As twilight casts a silver glow,
We gather close, we warm and stow.
The frosty front, the way we flow,
With memories bright in winter's show.

Tales from the Snowy Battleground

In the arena of snowy bliss,
Each snowball tells a tale, not amiss.
With every throw, a flurry of kiss,
In playful war, a joyous abyss.

The frigid air, it buzzes loud,
Under the shouts, we dance like a crowd.
A chorus builds, proud and unbowed,
In frosty gear, we clutch our shroud.

Flags of white grace every hill,
As laughter rises, we chase the thrill.
Friends and foes, a charming frill,
In every winter chill, we find the will.

As darkness wraps, we gather 'round,
Hot chocolate brews, a warming sound.
With cheeks aglow and hearts unbound,
The snowy tales from fun abound!

Shards of Ice

In the icy park we stand,
Lobbing snow with frozen hands.
Laughter echoes, spirits soar,
As snowballs fly, we keep the score.

A sneaky toss, a clever ruse,
My aim is sharp, it's yours to lose.
A fluffy blur, a comical plight,
Faces pelted in pure delight.

Chasing shadows, quick and spry,
Time escapes, and so do I.
Under piles of snowy bliss,
Victory's sweet, but so is this!

But who will win this frosty round?
With laughter loud, and joy unbound.
We'll leave our worries far behind,
In chilly fun, our hearts aligned.

Cold Conflict

Armed with snow, we take our stand,
Under the watch of winter's hand.
A smirk, a wink, then brave we charge,
In this cold war, we'll take it large.

Splats of white paint the winter's floor,
Giggles rush from every core.
A missed shot leads to fits of glee,
Like penguins sliding, wild and free.

Snowballs fly, a fluffy brigade,
On slippery slopes, our plans cascade.
With red noses and cheeks aglow,
We battle on, through frost and snow.

In the haze of laughter bright,
We forge ahead, no end in sight.
With a wink and a playful shove,
We'll freeze this fun, come winter's love.

Winter's Fractured Peace

In the hush of winter's chill,
Snow drifts softly, a perfect fill.
But chaos brews with stormy might,
As we prepare for a friendly fight.

Aiming snowballs with crafty glee,
Dodging bombs like artillery.
It's a battlefield with flurry bright,
Winter's peace is now a flight!

A wobbly throw and laughter roars,
As snowflakes tangle in wild chores.
This frozen feud, a riotous scene,
With friends aplenty, we reign supreme.

When cheeks are red and spirits high,
We'll conquer the cold, under the sky.
Though icy truce may soon ensue,
These chuckled battles always renew.

Slippery Showdown

On this snowy stage we brawl,
With laughter ringing, we give our all.
A precision toss, oh what fun,
A playful war that's just begun.

Faces bright and hearts so bold,
Each snowball crafted, each story told.
With mittens flapping, we take our cue,
In this frosty arena, shadows hue.

A slip and slide, a comical flare,
Down we tumble, without a care.
Joyful screams, the thrill of flight,
Beneath the stars, our spirits ignite.

So gather 'round when winter calls,
For these epic clashes, each hero falls.
With laughter ringing clear and loud,
We swipe at snow beneath the crowd.

Snowball Symphonies

In the frosty air we plot,
Snowballs ready, no second thought,
Laughter echoes, full of cheer,
Winter's magic, drawing near.

Aiming high, oh, what a sight!
Dodge and weave with all your might,
Here comes one, oh what a throw!
Lands atop a hat, a show!

With every toss, the giggles swell,
A frozen blast, we can't repel,
Cocoa waits for us to land,
Mittens warmed by a friendly hand.

As the sun dips, we cheer with glee,
Snowflakes dance, wild and free,
The day has closed, our joy ignites,
Memories bloom in snowy delights.

Winter Wilds

In the snowy woods, we dash,
Crafting ammo with great panache,
A secret stash beneath the snow,
Preparing for our wild show.

Whipping snowballs, quick and sly,
One hits Bob, oh my, oh my!
Laughter erupts, it's quite a scene,
Winter fun, where we've all been.

Chasing friends, we slip and slide,
Face full of snow, no place to hide,
Friends and foes, a playful plight,
Giggles burst in pure delight.

The sun now sets, what a day!
We pack it up and drift away,
But tomorrow, be aware,
We'll be back with snowy flair!

Flavors of Frost

White fluff balls flying like sweets,
Hit the mark, oh such fun feats,
A taste of cold that can't be beat,
Snowball flavors, oh so neat.

Blueberry here, a chocolate chip,
Splat goes Tim with a frosty whip,
Flavors burst, no time to stall,
Silly faces, we'll take them all.

Around the trees our laughter flows,
Joy and warmth, when cold wind blows,
The flavors mix with every throw,
Winter treats in an icy glow.

The day winds down, our count is high,
We'll dream of snow beneath the sky,
Flavors of frost, like ice cream divine,
In our hearts, with friends, we shine.

Hurling Happiness

Gathered close, with spirits bright,
Hurling joy, a pure delight,
Snowballs fly through the crisp, cold air,
Each one tossed, without a care.

Sticky gloves and rosy cheeks,
A sneak attack, Clyde just squeaks,
Caught off guard, his laughter rings,
In this chill, our joy springs.

The wildest game in the winter sun,
Dashing about, oh what fun!
Every fling brings a roaring cheer,
Hurling happiness, year after year.

As the day ends, stories will grow,
Of snowball battles and frosty show,
With each laugh shared, a love profound,
In these snowy realms, joy is found.

Snowbound Showdown

In the yard, a fortress stands tall,
Laughter erupts at the first snowball.
Aim and throw, a youthful delight,
Giggles echo through the frosty night.

Sneaky moves by our brave crew,
Behind a tree, a stealthy view.
Tossing flakes like a champion's game,
Chased down, then I felt the same.

But someone slipped on an ice patch,
Down they go, what a funny catch!
Snowflakes dance like confetti bright,
While we're lost in this snowy fight.

We stumble, we fall, we slip and glide,
Rolling snowballs as we chuck aside.
A snowbound showdown, pure bliss abounds,
Each laugh we share, the best moment found.

Icicle Avengers

With icicles sharp, we take our stand,
Heroes of winter, a quirky band.
Shouting names like brave crusaders,
Daring acts, just like the creators.

Snowballs fly with a whoosh and thud,
Aiming for foes, creating a flood.
Turning the yard into a battlefield,
Snowy shields are our only shield.

One brave friend makes a surprise attack,
Hits me right on the back!
A snowball burst with giggling spree,
We roll with laughter, wild and free.

Icicle Avengers unite with might,
Joyful chaos lights up the night.
In the madness, we find our cheer,
The weirdest battles happen here.

Powdery Ambush

Under the trees we scurry and hide,
With powdery ammo, we plan our stride.
Ambush in winter, stealth on the go,
Ready to pounce, like a sneaky snow.

The whispers rise, 'It's time to strike!'
And then laughter erupts from a nearby hike.
Caught off guard, they scramble to flee,
Frosty faces turn bright with glee.

With guided frostballs, we take aim,
Each one is thrown like it's part of the game.
Although I missed, my friend fell down,
Snowy clichés wrapped in laughter's gown.

Victory or loss? It matters so little,
When we're bundled up, it's all just a riddle.
A powdery ambush, wrapped in delight,
Snowy skirmishes marking our night.

Arctic Clash

In the blistering cold, we gather 'round,
An arctic clash, where joy is found.
Snowballs shape like marshmallows light,
A friendly brawl, what a silly sight!

With smiles wide, we rain down the white,
Tossing laughter with each frosty fight.
Bouncing off cheeks, the snow takes flight,
Every throw sparks pure delight.

Friends become foes in this icy spree,
Allies turn sneaky just for under me.
Down goes the king, oh what a fall!
Who knew a snowball could bring such a squall?

As snowflakes swirl in the chilly air,
We dance in chaos, without a care.
In the end, it's the fun we relate,
An arctic clash, sealing our fate.

Shivering Shenanigans

In the yard, snowballs form,
Laughter echoes, hearts are warm.
Dodging projectiles, swift and quick,
A friendly battle, a frosty trick.

Snowflakes dance upon our hats,
Giggles spill like chubby cats.
A sneaky throw, just out of sight,
Oh, what fun, a snowy fight!

Cold noses press against the glass,
As winter warriors boldly pass.
With foam and fluff, they take their aim,
Who knew this chill would spark such fame?

Now soaked and shivering, what a sight,
Winners claim their snowy bite.
The endgame's near, but who is best?
We leave with joy, no time for rest.

Arctic Adventures

With sleds and shouts, we roam the hill,
Winter's magic, oh what a thrill!
Snowmen watch with buttons for eyes,
As we launch balls, a sweet surprise.

Amid the chaos, we share a grin,
Cold cheeks warm from laughter within.
A catapult made from a sturdy branch,
Our summer rival, we try to branch.

Caught off guard, a snowball flies,
Right into mom's porch, oh, the cries!
Yet with a twinkle, she grins so wide,
Joining the fight, she'll be our guide.

As the sun sets and shadows grow,
An end to our antics, time to go.
With rosy cheeks and stories to tell,
Winter's pranks, we know them well.

Snowy Mischief

Fluffy clouds, the sky turns white,
Friends gather round, ready to fight.
Puffs of snow fly through the air,
Giggles burst forth, oh what a scare!

A snowball skims my sister's cap,
She spins around, sets her trap.
With envy brewing, I take aim,
Revenge is sweet, a snowy game.

Shovels wielded like swords so fine,
We plot and scheme, with snow we align.
The dog barks, confusion unfolds,
Chasing snowballs, brave and bold.

As daylight fades, we start to tire,
No more energy, but hearts on fire.
A promise made, we'll come again,
Next winter's bliss, our friendly reign.

Frosty Fancies

In frosty air, we jump and shout,
The world is ours, there's no doubt.
Twists and turns with snowflakes bright,
We craft our plans, ready to fight.

A stealthy sneak behind the tree,
Wait for the moment, just let it be.
With wild throws, we scatter fast,
Time flies by, but we have a blast.

Sledding down that hill, oh so steep,
Laughter resonates, no time for sleep.
Snow muffles sound — all is serene,
Then chaos erupts, an icy scene!

Cold and wet, with red cheeks aglow,
We pack our bags, it's time to go.
Though the day ends, we had our fun,
We'll meet again when winter's come!

Carefree Chaos

In the park we gather wide,
Laughter echoes, hearts collide.
Snowballs fly with playful glee,
Winter's war is wild and free.

Chasing friends, we slip and fall,
Landing softly, laughter's call.
Frosty faces, cheeks aglow,
Victory dances in the snow.

Snowflakes cling to woolen caps,
When the air's filled with loud claps.
We shout and shout, we cheer and tease,
Each round's a riot, such a breeze!

Even moms in coats abound,
Join the fray, their joy unbound.
Suddenly, a snowball flies!
Oops! A friendly surprise!

Spherical Skirmish

Round and round the snowballs soar,
Each one packed, we crave for more.
Team A laughs, Team B yells loud,
Spherical warfare, snowmen proud.

Caught off-guard, then counter-strike,
Watch your back, it's like a hike!
Dashing here, then sliding there,
Snowball battle fills the air.

With clumps of white in every hand,
We build our forts, we take our stand.
Snowmen guard with frosty eyes,
As we fight 'neath winter skies.

But wait! A truce? Oh what a treat!
Hot cocoa starts our grand repeat.
The skirmish ceases, laughter twirls,
Friendship blooms in icy swirls.

Blinding Brights

Under skies so crisp and bright,
Snowflakes shimmer, pure delight.
Wear a scarf and laugh with cheer,
Here comes a snowball! Duck, oh dear!

Hats and gloves thrown every place,
Accidental frosty face.
Giggles erupt like bursting plans,
Amidst the chaos, friendly spans.

Whirling snowballs twist and twirl,
As we leap and twine and swirl.
In blinding white, we lose the goal,
All's fair in the winter's toll!

When the sun begins to set,
We gather up, no signs of fret.
From frozen fun, our hearts ignite,
In snowy laughter, pure delight.

Dancing with Drifts

Snowflakes drift like music light,
We gather 'round, our spirits bright.
Arms extended, ready to fling,
Our laughter in the air takes wing.

Each snowball flies, a perfect curve,
Joy in every bounce and swerve.
Kids and grown-ups, all in sync,
A wintry ball, a playful rink.

Frosty fingers, rosy cheeks,
On the ground, victory speaks.
We glide and slip, fall with flair,
In snowy drifts without a care.

As snowmen cheer and trees applaud,
We dance along, the frosty God.
In winter's charm, all cares remain,
Wrapped in joy, we dance again.

Frozen Memories of a Whirlwind Duel

In the yard, a chill in the air,
Laughter erupts, without a care.
Snowballs fly, a frosty blast,
Friends and foes, memories cast.

A round of giggles, a dodge and weave,
In this battle, who would believe?
Woolen hats tilted, cheeks aglow,
Victory declared, but oh, the snow!

We crouch behind mounds, like little spies,
With sneaky grins and gleeful eyes.
Aiming true, the snowball's flight,
Who knew winter could feel so right?

The dog joins in, a snowball tease,
Chasing snowflakes, with such ease.
This frozen war, a sight to behold,
Our snug distress in the winter cold.

Cascades of Joy in a Winter Wonderland

Snowflakes tumble, a soft ballet,
Joyful chaos, let the games play.
With laughter ringing, we gather round,
Cascading fun, the joy we've found.

Armored with layers, bundled tight,
We charge ahead, ready to fight.
A flurry of missiles, aimed with glee,
Chasing the giggles, wild and free.

The moment paused, a breathless cheer,
As snowballs collide, that's the frontier!
Mittens soaked, but spirits high,
A truce declared as the snow softly sighs.

Frozen treasures, snowmen stand tall,
While laughter lingers over all.
Echoes of joy in the crisp, cool air,
These winter days, we'll always share.

Winter's Frosty Duel

Gathered together, our feet all numb,
Ready for battle, oh here we come!
With snowballs packed, a flying spree,
In this frosty duel, we are wild and free.

Tumbles and slips, oh what a sight,
Friendships flourish in the winter light.
Cold noses wrinkle, and hearts race fast,
Each frosty skirmish is built to last.

The starry sky, a backdrop bright,
As laughter dances through the night.
At each snowball's crumple, joy unfolds,
In this winter tale, our youth retold!

Snow forts arise, a fortress stout,
Smiling soldiers, of this there's no doubt.
With each snowy fight, the bonds we bloom,
In the heart of the frost, there's no room for gloom.

Whispers of Flurries

Gentle whispers of flurries fall,
In this wintry world, we heed the call.
With bundled laughter, we take our stance,
In a playful duel, we twirl and dance.

Snowflakes swirl, a magical scene,
As each frosty fling finds its mean.
Gleeful shouts fill the nipping air,
Underneath trees, our carefree lair.

Cold fingers toss a cheeky ball,
With every dodge, we heed our all.
Giggles echo, a symphony sweet,
In this snowy haven, joy can't be beat.

As twilight settles, the battles cease,
In the glow of warmth, we find our peace.
These frosty memories, so close and dear,
Whispers of flurries, we'll always cheer!

Snowy Showdown

In the field so white and bright,
Snowballs fly with all their might.
Laughter echoes, spirits soar,
As snowmen tumble, what a chore!

Packs of ice, a clever art,
Dodging skills, they play a part.
Cheeks are rosy, noses cold,
Friends unite, both young and old.

The dog joins in, a furry whiz,
Chasing snowballs, what a biz!
Clouds of laughter, smiles abound,
Victory claimed, without a sound!

As the day fades, snowflakes fall,
We head on home, enthralled by all.
With chilly toes and tales to tell,
Of snowy battles, we all fell!

Niveous Nuisance

Snowflakes dance, a whimsical sight,
Turning our world to pure delight.
But oh, what's this? A sneaky throw,
Right in the face! The laughter flows.

Warriors clad in coats so thick,
Launching projectiles, oh so quick!
But one slips down, a perfect score,
As snowballs splatter and children roar.

The sleds collide, a glorious crash,
Tumbling giggles, a comical splash.
Eyes wide open, a prank's in store,
Sneaky whispers, then count to four!

In the chaos, friendships bloom,
Snow forts rise, dispelling gloom.
With every throw and playful chat,
We find joy in snowy combat!

Winter's Wrath

White blanket drapes the world so still,
Nature's splendor, an icy thrill.
But chaos brews on this fun-filled day,
As snowballs launch in a feathery ballet.

Pelted faces, it's all in good fun,
Chasing each other 'til the day is done.
Giggles echo, the temperature drops,
Snowflakes fall and the laughter pops.

Mittens wet and boots all soaked,
Children gather, plans are poked.
The battle rages, smiles are wide,
Every throw, a taunting ride!

As sunlight fades, the fun won't stop,
With frozen mittens and excitement on top.
We plot our revenge by night's soft glow,
With dreams of snowmen and more snow to throw!

Flake-tastrophe

In deep drifts, the mischief brews,
Snowball launches, we join the crew.
Check your aim, prepare to flee,
For every hit brings more glee!

Friends conspire in fluffy hats,
Building forts with clever chats.
But watch your back, here comes a team,
With snowy puffs and a snowy scheme.

Giggles and shouts fill the air,
A flake-tastrophe, beware, beware!
Belly flops and playful dives,
In this winter, our laughter thrives.

As dusk approaches, we head for home,
With aching cheeks and hearts that roam.
These frosty tales, so warmly told,
Will spark our joy when the nights are cold!

Hurling Hope

Snowflakes drift like dreams,
Laughter fills the air,
Little balls of icy glee,
With each toss, we share.

Aiming at the rivals,
With a mischievous grin,
Whispers of sweet revenge,
Let the games begin!

Furry hats and mittens,
Fly through the bright blue,
Slippery paths of chaos,
Watch your step, it's true!

Victory in the distance,
Snowmen cheer us on,
But the truth is, my dear friends,
We all end up in prawn!

Winter's Wager

A mound of snow awaits,
Who's brave enough to start?
With scheming little packages,
It's a frosty work of art.

Socks get drenched in laughter,
As missiles whiz and zing,
The cold bites at our noses,
Yet joy makes our hearts sing.

Goggles slip down clumsily,
When we make a wild throw,
Cheeks red from all the giggles,
Dodging flurries like a pro!

Snowball battles rage on,
With hot cocoa on the side,
We wager our next snack,
For this fun, we take pride!

Tales of the Chill

Once upon a snow day,
We plotted like great kings,
Battles fought in silence,
My, the joy this brings!

Beneath a white confetti,
The laughter hides so well,
Who knew a snow-packed ball,
Could cast such warmth and swell?

Fur coats and big boots,
Are summoned to the fray,
A flurry of the fanciful,
In a glorious ballet.

As if in winter's circus,
We twirl around in glee,
Until we slip, fall, and roll,
Now that's our victory!

Merry Misadventures

Today's the day for chaos,
We gear up, brace for fun,
With every icy projectile,
The games have just begun.

Giggles echo loudly,
As snowballs fly and burst,
Navigating snowdrifts,
Adventure's always first!

Aiming for the neighbor,
Missed! And hit the dog,
Now he's in the mayhem,
Jumping like a frog!

So bring on the mischief,
Let's create snow-filled memes,
With each snowy explosion,
We're living out our dreams!

Frostbitten Fury

In winter's grip, we took our stance,
With frozen hands, we dared to dance.
Laughter echoed, as snowballs flew,
A frosty fight, just me and you.

A slippery slope was our battlefield,
With icy tactics, we would not yield.
Each throw a giggle, each dodge a cheer,
Snowflakes spinning, we had no fear.

But then it happened, a slip, a trip,
Down I went with a frosty flip.
You aimed so well, it hit my head,
Now snow's my blanket, laying in bed.

Now with a grin, we end this spree,
Next time I'll bring a cup of hot tea.
For every snowball with cheeky glee,
Comes laughter shared in winter's spree.

Flakes of Discord

In the yard beneath the winter sun,
We gathered snow, this would be fun.
Laughter rang as we built our fright,
A fortress made for snowball fight.

But alliances changed with every throw,
Friends turned foes in the frosty glow.
A blizzard of giggles, and shouts of glee,
Dodging and weaving like wild, carefree.

A miscalculated toss led to a crash,
Snow up my nose, eyes in a splash.
You laughed out loud, what a silly sight,
One for the books, this chaotic night.

As daylight wanes, our battles cease,
Trade snowballs for cocoa, a sweet little peace.
With smiles and warmth, we'll call it a day,
Until next time, when we'll laugh and play.

Battle in the Snow

With winter whispers, the challenge began,
Snowballs stacked high by every young man.
A count of three, and away we flew,
In this frosty brawl, there was much to do.

Amid the laughter, a snowball flies,
An unsuspecting friend lets out a sigh.
Thwacked on the noggin, the snow flew wide,
Drenched and delighted, we laughed with pride.

Yet some were crafty, with tricks up their sleeves,
A snowman formed, with goals to achieve.
"Defend the fortress!" someone did shout,
As the snowballs whizzed, with no time to doubt.

With darkness approaching, the fight wore thin,
We rolled in the drifts, tumbled, fell in.
A snowball truce as the sun tucked away,
With fond memories, we'll return one day.

Chilling Skirmish

The air was crisp, perfect for a fray,
We donned our gear, the kids yelled hooray.
Snowflakes danced as we planned our scheme,
Outside the window, we'd form a dream.

With a sneaky throw and a giggling pout,
I aimed for you, but hit someone out.
The crowd erupted, oh what a sight,
Laughter exploding in pure delight.

But oh the mischief, beware the prank,
A snowball shower from the new kid's flank.
We ducked and we rolled, avoiding the flurry,
Sprinting for cover, it got a bit blurry.

As daylight faded, the battle grew chill,
We gathered our troops, with laughter to spill.
A hot cocoa toast, to the fun that we shared,
For in winter's grasp, we showed we all dared.

Powdered Rivalries Beneath the Sky

In the field, a mound takes shape,
A ball of frost, a snowman's cape.
With mischief brewed and giggles loud,
We gear up now, a rebel crowd.

A sly sneak up, a launch so bold,
Aiming at friends, both young and old.
Direct hit lands, laughter explodes,
As snowflakes flutter down like codes.

The chase ensues, round and round,
With each new toss, our bonds are found.
Through piles of snow, we run amok,
Creating chaos, our shared luck.

At winter's heart, we stand in ranks,
As iceballs fly, we share our pranks.
United in laughter, we feel so spry,
In powdered rivalries that reach the sky.

Snow-Covered Conquests

With every throw, the grudge begins,
It's icy war, let laughter spin.
Clumps of white fly through the air,
Foundations of joy, beyond compare.

A fortress built from snow so bright,
Defended fiercely, oh what a sight!
With friends as foes and glee unfurled,
We take our stand against the world.

A snowball lands with a whack and crack,
As red-cheeked faces hold nothing back.
Puffs of cold in playful blights,
As camaraderie ignites the nights.

Together we fall in squeals of delight,
Tumbling 'neath stars in the frosty night.
With every laugh, our spirits soar,
In snow-covered conquests, we crave for more!

Laughter Amidst the Snowdrifts

Rolling in flakes, the fun begins,
We wage our wars with squealing grins.
A perfect aim? Quite the aimless plight,
As friends collide, oh what a sight!

Pockets stuffed with snowy balls,
Honeycomb laughs, as everyone falls.
Surprise attack from out of blue,
We can't stop laughing, what else to do?

Catching our breath, then ready we stand,
Strategizing, it's all unplanned.
The snowstorm rages, our laughter streams,
In this crazy world of winter dreams.

Together, we tumble through winter's glow,
In a snow-covered world, just let it flow.
From each fluffy pile, joy ignites,
In laughter and frolic, oh what delights!

Icebound Adventures of Winter Warriors

At dawn we gather, our troops align,
With scarves wrapped tight, we're feeling fine.
We launch our rounds, full of glee,
Each icy ball flies wild and free.

Slips and slides amidst the fun,
With laughter rippling under the sun.
Our homemade ammo, a sight to see,
Laughter echoes, pure jubilee.

In madcap skirmishes, we engage,
As chilly antics fly off the page.
Winter warriors with hearts ablaze,
In snowdrifts rich, we're set to amaze.

The day winds down, but memories last,
With every snowball, a shared blast.
Amongst the ice, our spirits roar,
In icebound adventures, we seek for more!

Winter Whispers in the Air

Snowflakes twirl, with glee they dart,
Chasing friends, a playful art.
Laughter echoes, muffled cheers,
In winter's grip, we cast our fears.

A snowball whizzes, aimed so true,
Missed the mark, and splat! Right through!
Giggles erupt as we all fall,
In a frosty heap, we have a ball.

Red noses and cheeks frozen bright,
Plotting revenge in the soft twilight.
Sneaky ambush behind a tree,
Prepare to launch, just wait and see.

When the day ends, we're cold and wet,
Yet the memories linger, we won't forget.
With hearts so warm, despite the chill,
Winter's joy, a thrill we'll fulfill.

Frosty Battles Unleashed

Dressed in layers, we take our stand,
Snowballs ready, it's time to band.
A trumpet call, the battle begins,
With laughter and grit, we're serious twins.

A soft projectile flies through the air,
And hits a buddy, jokes to share.
"Hey, that's cheating!" shouts a friend,
With playful grins, the fun won't end.

Teammates scatter, a snow white swoop,
Like stealthy ninjas, we form a group.
Sneaky tactics, we break apart,
But snowballs fly straight from the heart.

When the sun sets, and puffs of steam,
We lie back, just living the dream.
With snowflakes melting on tired cheeks,
Laughter's warmth is what winter seeks.

Flurries of Laughter and Ice

In a world of white, our joys collide,
With snowballs packed, we take the ride.
Quick as a wink, they'll catapult,
Sending giggles like an adult's jolt.

A fierce volley, then someone slips,
Down they go, with flailing hips.
Rolling laughter, stuck in the snow,
A winter wonder, with spirits aglow.

Sleds are flying down the hill,
Somehow we end up with a thrill.
'Tis not just ice, it's the friendships gained,
In this frosty realm, fun's uncontained.

As shadows stretch and day turns dusk,
Huddled close, together we trust.
With snowflakes swirling, our hearts light and free,
It's a winter tale of camaraderie.

Snowflakes and Rivalries

A pile of snow, a fortress of dreams,
Rivalries spark, or so it seems.
With each frozen chunk, we scheme and plan,
As winter unfolds, it becomes our span.

"Team Snowballs!" we cheer with zest,
But our laughter reveals who is best.
A rogue snowball, a sudden strike,
A snowball battle? Oh, what a hike!

Jeers and jests fly like our snow,
With playful fire, we tackle the show.
Friendships tested on this frosty sea,
In these winter wars, we're wild and free.

As darkness falls and battles cease,
Round the fire, we find our peace.
With stories shared and snacks in tow,
The best of times are the ones we know.

Antarctic Altercations

In the white expanse, we make our stand,
With icy missiles in trembling hand.
Laughter erupts, the cold bites deep,
As snowballs soar and tactics leap.

Aimed at faces, no one takes aim,
Running and dodging, it's all a game.
Giggles that echo, a chill in the air,
Who's the next target? Come catch if you dare!

The snowman guards our snowy domain,
As we pack and launch in this frosty campaign.
But oh, the surprise of a soft clump,
A friendly hit from a hidden lump!

With piles of fluff, we let laughter fly,
Each toss is met with a shriek and a sigh.
Bows are drawn for the final round,
In the battle of jokes where joy abounds.

Snowbound Surprises

Beneath the drifting flakes we play,
Crafting missiles to our dismay.
A blizzard of laughter in the crisp cool air,
As snowballs fly without a care.

With a stealthy step, I sneak around,
Only to trip on unseen ground.
A face full of snow! Oh, what a sight!
The funniest skirmish we'll talk about tonight.

Two foes collide and tumble down,
Clouds of white envelop the town.
The squirrels watch in utter glee,
As we chase each other, wild and free.

A surprise attack from behind a tree,
Pelted in powder, oh, woe is me!
Yet we all collapse, laughing so loud,
In this wonderland, we're foolish and proud.

Frosty High Jinks

With hats askew and noses bright,
We strategize in the snowball fight.
Armed with fluff, on this frozen field,
We're warriors of laughter, no need to yield.

Snowflakes tumble, our joy takes flight,
A swift little snowball launched just right.
But when shields fail, we laugh and cheer,
For a hit is a victory, let's make it clear!

Turning our backs, plotting a sneak,
Just watch out for the snowy sneak peak!
A throw gone wrong leads to fits of glee,
A frozen foe slides down the tree.

Dodging and weaving, we're kings and queens,
In this land of snow, where silliness gleans.
The sunshine glimmers on frosty fun,
As friends unite, we're never outdone.

Frozen Capers

As ice and snow create a stage,
We dive into antics, a brand-new age.
With every throw, a twinkle in our eyes,
Creating a scene that's sure to surprise.

Encircled by snow, we dance and prance,
Everyone eager to take a chance.
Laughing hard as we plot and scheme,
In the midst of chaos, we're living the dream.

From unexpected falls to slippery slides,
The frosty landscape becomes our guides.
With each snowball sent, joy multiplies,
Filling the air with our echoes and cries.

Yet beware the moment when friends unite,
To churn out snowballs in victorious flight!
For in this caper, where fortunes can change,
From laughter to snow, our antics are strange.

Battle of the Frost

In a field of white, we all take aim,
Laughter erupts, it's all a game.
Snowballs fly through the brisk, cold air,
Dodge if you can, if you dare!

Aiming for faces, what a silly sight,
Flurries of balls, a comical fight.
With every hit, giggles cascade,
A truce is declared—let's make a snow maid!

Hats askew, we charge with glee,
Wipe your brow, is that snow or pee?
A frost-kissed face and frozen toes,
But the laughter lingers, it only grows.

As dusk approaches, we gather near,
Sharing hot cocoa, spreading cheer.
The best of battles, with friends in tow,
A winter's tale we'll forever know.

Icy Encounters

Two foes meet on a frosty field,
Snowball battle, the fun revealed.
With a crafty grin and sly little squint,
Prepare for impact, you'll feel the glint!

Friends turn foes in this snowy bout,
A flurry of missiles, there's no doubt.
Laughter spills like frozen streams,
As we create our winter dreams.

Every throw is a daring feat,
Clumps of powder beneath our feet.
Who will win? We laugh and cheer,
At this crazy game we hold so dear.

When the day ends and we're soaked to the bone,
We gather our gear, let's head back home.
With rosy cheeks and warmth in our hearts,
It's not just the snow, it's the laughter that starts.

Tempestuous Toss

A wild wind blows, it's jackets on tight,
Ready to battle beneath pale moonlight.
The sound of laughter fills the scene,
As we launch our snowballs, oh so mean!

Aim for the target, but miss by a mile,
And hit your buddy—oh, what a style!
Yelling, "You missed!" with a playful pout,
We charge again, no time for doubt.

With shiny cheeks and laughter anew,
We roll the snow, constructing our crew.
Snow forts are built, troops getting bold,
Victory dances in the winter cold.

As snowflakes fall, we gather around,
The best of memories, let's get unbound!
With giggles and shouts, we'll never tire,
These icy encounters, we truly admire.

Powder-Packed Rivalry

On the hilltop, a battle's begun,
With laughter and shouts, oh, what fun!
Snowballs form like little white threats,
Each one tossed, no one forgets.

Running and slipping, a slippery strife,
With frosty hands, we all love this life.
The thrill of the throw, the joy of the hit,
Dodging like pros, while we all fit!

Victory sweetens with every missed chance,
Snowflakes swirling, inviting a dance.
With cheeks all aglow from the cold winter's bite,
Our friendship and laughter, the true highlight.

As we trudge home, soaked and all smiles,
We gather our stories and share for a while.
In this powder-packed rivalry, we find delight,
A winter wonderland, our hearts feel so light.

The Great Frost Flurry Tactics

In winter's chill, they gather round,
With frosty balls upon the ground.
Laughter echoes in the air,
As they plan their snowy affair.

One sneaks low, a sneaky ghost,
While others cheer, they love to boast.
Snowflakes drift, a soft ballet,
A flurry of fun in bright display.

The snowballs fly, a whizzing blur,
Bouncing off hats, a chilly stir.
Allies laugh, their cheeks all red,
As snowflakes dance above their heads.

With each thrown ball, a shout of glee,
This wintry war, oh joy, you see!
And when it ends, not a winner found,
They're all just friends, forever bound.

Whimsical War in Winter's Realm

In a land where snowflakes gleam so bright,
Children clash in a frosty fight.
Giggles erupt as they take their aim,
In this playful, snowy game.

Little feet in boots do race,
Across the field, a frozen space.
Snowballs soar with laughter loud,
Each one tossed, a cheerful cloud.

A tumble here, a slip and slide,
Rolling down with arms spread wide.
In every flurry, a tale to tell,
Of clumsy knights who fell so well.

When sun dips low and shadows creep,
They gather 'round, their secrets to keep.
With pink-nosed smiles and hearts so light,
They vow to meet for another fight.

Chilling Rivalries and Frozen Fables

In the frosty air, a showdown brews,
With piles of snow, and playful ruse.
Snowballs fly, a winter spree,
As laughter rings, so wild and free.

Two teams form, each one thinks bold,
Fabled rivalries from tales of old.
With sneaky stunts and crafty plays,
They cheer and chant through snowy days.

A rogue snowball takes a flight,
And then it lands—a goofy sight!
A hat lost here, a glove misplaced,
In this chill, there's no time to waste.

When the sky turns gray and dusk sets in,
They shake cold hands, a warm grin.
For in this wintry, playful brawl,
Friendships grow, a joy for all.

A Festival of Snowy Skirmishes

In a festival of snow, joy leaps wide,
As children gather, no need to hide.
With snowballs packed in every palm,
The world is wrapped in winter's calm.

A strategic throw lands on a hat,
A chuckle erupts—it's a joyous spat!
The snowflakes twinkle like glittering stars,
As laughter rings out from near and far.

Each launch a chance for playful mayhem,
With squeals of delight that no one can stem.
Frosty face-off, a battle so bright,
In the heart of winter, what pure delight!

When twilight falls, and battles cease,
They gather round, sharing peace.
Snowy skirmishes turn into tales,
Of frosty fun that always prevails.

Whirlwind of White

Hats askew, a laugh erupts,
Snowballs fly like playful pups.
Laughter dances through the air,
Victory's sweet, but who would dare?

Frosty cheeks and frozen toes,
Aiming well, who really knows?
Giggles echo, quite absurd,
As snowballs fly, they flip and twirled.

A brave heart claims the snowy throne,
Yet trip and slip, they're all alone.
Losing ground while gaining cheer,
The snowstorm's laughter is sincere.

With every toss, a friendship grows,
In frozen fields, the fun just flows.
A war of giggles, joy takes flight,
In this whirlwind of pure delight.

Flurry Frenzy

Out in the cold, we set the stage,
With fluffy ammo, we engage.
A perfect throw, or is it luck?
Missed the target, and now we're stuck!

Faces bright, with snowflakes crowned,
A comical dance, slipping around.
Dive for cover, laughter's the plan,
Snowballs fly, but I can't stand!

In a snowy clash, we spark delight,
Who's in danger? Who's in sight?
An icy thunder, the game is on,
And with each toss, we quietly fawn.

Frenzy swirls, and joys collide,
In fluffy chaos, we bide our time.
When winter's chill meets laughter's spree,
What fun it is, just you and me!

Glacial Gambit

Chilly fingers, a sneaky plot,
Prepare yourself, it's gonna be hot!
Snowballs packed in perfect form,
Watch out friends, the storm is born!

Strategic throws, a crafty aim,
But oops! My shoe's caught in the game.
As I slip and smack the ground,
A snowball lands without a sound!

Darting here, a twist of fate,
With laughter loud, we cannot wait.
Friends unite, our battle grows,
As flurries fly, and giggles blow.

In this icy plot, we find our place,
With every throw, we share a space.
A frosty triumph, warmly spun,
Through frozen fun, we've just begun!

Snowy Rivalries

Sleds and shouts, the race begins,
Snowy armor, let's be friends.
No time for worries, just have fun,
In snowy rivalries, we won't shun.

Laughter's riddle, who will prevail?
A fluff-ball hits with a comical flail.
Get ready folks, the stakes are high,
Who will conquer? Who will sigh?

In icy rounds, we dare to dream,
Watch your back, it's quite the scheme.
But as we slip and tumble down,
We win together, each in a crown!

So let the games of winter play,
With every toss, we'll find our way.
In friendship's warmth, we'll always meet,
In snowy rivalries, life's a treat!

Snowstorm Showdown

In the yard where laughter roars,
Kids are scheming behind the doors.
Snowballs packed with glee on hand,
Ready to form a frosty band.

With a sly grin, a throw takes flight,
Laughter echoes into the night.
Frosty missiles zip and zoom,
As snowflakes dance like in a cartoon.

One hits a tree, a powdery burst,
So frantic now, they break the first.
Chasing friends, their cheeks all red,
It's all in fun, no tears to shed.

Then from the sky, a snowy drift,
Moms yell, "Time for a warm-up shift!"
Every heart is light and bright,
As they retreat from the playful fight.

Flurry Brawl

Giggling troops in a snowy land,
Plotting mischief, oh so grand.
Each snowball formed with crafty care,
Aiming high, they scale the air.

A whistling shot goes askew and wild,
Tumbles a snowman, oh, what a child!
With arms outstretched, it cries, "No fair!"
The laughter spreads everywhere.

Caught in the crossfire, a cat dashes,
Through the crowd, the snowball splashes.
With each throw, a fit of giggles,
Winter wonderland filled with wiggles.

Time flies by, as snowmen stand,
Peace returns to the winter land.
With memories bright, they wave goodbye,
Until next time, the snowflakes fly!

Blizzard Barrage

Whirling snowflakes in the chilly air,
Kids grab snowballs with the utmost flair.
A gathering storm, oh what a sight,
As giggling squads prepare for fight.

One strategic toss and a target's found,
Victory cheers in playful sound.
Moments of triumph, then quick retreat,
Drenched in laughter, their hearts skip a beat.

In the frenzy, a snowball mishit,
Right in the face, oh what a hit!
His comrades chuckle, but he's plotting,
Just wait till he starts his snowball dotting.

As the sun dips down, all frozen and sore,
They trudge back home, wanting just more.
For tomorrow unfolds a brand new day,
When winter's game brings cheers into play.

Chill Breeze Rivalry

In the backyard, a kingdom of snow,
The air is crisp, and cheeks aglow.
Strategies hatched like stealthy ninjas,
Excited voices, a thrill that lingers.

Snowballs forming, they're packing tight,
Taking aim, oh what a sight!
With a gentle toss, a friend goes down,
He rolls and laughs, the snowball crown.

A surprise attack from behind the bush,
Laughter erupts in a playful rush.
One by one, snowmen start to fall,
Victory cheers do echo for all.

But as the sun begins its descent,
They shake hands and share the content.
Fleeting moments, forever they'll hold,
In winters past, the tales retold.

Winter's Playground of Heroes

In coats so puffy, we gear up tight,
With snowballs ready, we spark delight.
Laughter echoes, the air's so fresh,
A barrage begins as we start to mesh.

Flakes in the air, they swirl and spin,
Some aim for the knee, but most land on skin.
Dodging and diving, we weave and crawl,
A well-placed throw and down goes Paul!

Giggles erupt, with each little hit,
In this winter kingdom, we don't ever quit.
Heroes we are, in our mismatched gear,
Crafting our memories, year after year.

As snowmen watch, with a frosty glare,
They judge our antics, but we do not care.
For in this playground, so wild and grand,
The frozen warfare is perfectly planned.

Aerial Assaults of Fluffy Projectiles

Amidst the trees where shadows play,
We gather round for a snowy fray.
With tiny hands, we build our stash,
Then launch our missiles with a glorious splash.

Watch out from above, the clouds cry 'snow!'
We hurl our fluff with a mighty blow.
Target acquired, and here comes that thud,
Oops, sorry buddy, that was your bud!

Cackling loudly, we start to plot,
A cunning strategy on the spot.
Fortresses built with walls of white,
Every throw painted with a sense of delight.

In this battlefield, giggles ensue,
Retreating soldiers call out for a brew.
But here we stay, prepared to wield,
More fluffy projectiles upon the field.

The Frosty Duelists' Dance

Two duelists face off, their brows all furrowed,
With snowballs gripped, their breath all burrowed.
At the count of three, let the fun begin,
Puff puffs of powder swirl all around like sin.

A dodging move, then a crafty roll,
Snowflakes collide with a tinkling toll.
One warrior slips; what a sight to see!
Laughter erupts, it's pure comedy.

The icy duel leads to friendly grins,
Chilled but cheerful, there are no sins.
For as they tumble in a comedic flair,
This frosty dance is beyond compare.

When the battle fades, the snowflakes sigh,
These frosty duelists have theories awry.
Together they sit, sharing tales of the fight,
As the sunset glows with a hint of twilight.

Snowbound Jesters and Warriors

Giggling jesters in their frozen quest,
Tumble and fumble in the snowy fest.
With each snowball that flies through the sky,
The gales of laughter ring out, oh my!

Warriors brave with cheeks all aglow,
Building their kingdoms with glittering snow.
But under the layers of frost and chill,
Lurk pranksters plotting for a sly kill.

An ambush awaits, hidden in plain sight,
As clumps of white await with delight.
With glee they attack, playfully spry,
Leaving no madcap without alibi.

In this snowy realm where laughter reigns,
Every chill moment wipes out the pains.
So gather your crew and join the parade,
For the snowbound jesters are never afraid!

Chilling Confrontations on Frosted Fields

Snowflakes swirl in the winter's breeze,
Laughter echoes, the kids take their knees.
With a wink and a grin, they plan their strike,
Snowballs fly fast, oh what a hike!

Aimed at the squirrels, oh what a sight,
They dodge and they dart, oh, what a delight!
But one brave lad, in his winter coat,
Takes a direct hit, and begins to gloat.

Now snow's in his hair, and he's starting to pout,
But with a quick laugh, he joins in the rout.
As laughter erupts, there's no room for shame,
This frosty adventure is all in the game!

The sun starts to set, the day's winding down,
With cheeks rosy red and each child a clown.
They march homeward, leaving behind
A battlefield of joy, oh, what a find!

Gleeful Chaos in the Snow

In a world of white, where snowflakes convene,
Kids gather round, in a jubilant scene.
With snow piled high, they craft their best,
A snowball brigade, prepared for a jest!

Laughter erupts like the snow from their hands,
The dance of the snowballs, no one understands.
Aiming at friends while dodging the flurries,
They tumble and roll, caught up in the wherries.

A snowball lands hard on a poor cat nearby,
It jumps in surprise, a confused little guy!
The kids all burst out, a fit of pure glee,
As the cat scoffs and climbs up a tree.

With snow down their backs and joy in their hearts,
They craft one last snowman before it departs.
As the day fades away, and the stars twinkle bright,
They vow to return for more frosty delight!

Frosty Feuds and Cheerful Chaos

With cheeks wreathed in red, they gather around,
In this wintery circus, where laughter is found.
Snowballs assembled like troops on parade,
Ready for battle, not one will evade!

The leader shouts loud, with a mischievous grin,
'Prepare for the onslaught, let the fun begin!'
Sister versus brother, teammates aligned,
In this quirky contest, true joy they will find.

The neighbor looks out, peeking from behind
His frosty old window, hoping to unwind.
But a snowball flies in, right through the pane,
And the chase is on, oh what glorious pain!

When night falls at last, and the fun has to cease,
Amid mounds of the snow, they find their peace.
With snowflakes still dancing, they sing with delight,
'Next year we'll return for another great fight!'

A Symphony of Snowbound Skirmishes

A chorus of giggles fills up the cold air,
As kids clutch their snowballs with stylish flair.
They plot and they strategize, ready to play,
In this frostbitten field where frolic holds sway.

With a thump and a thud, they hurl their white balls,
The laughter erupts like the sound of loud calls.
Old man Jenkins peeks from behind his own door,
Caught in the crossfire—what a lively war!

Snow forts are built with pride and with care,
As kids take their places, all feathers and flare.
The flag flies high on the biggest snow mound,
This whimsical stage is where joy will abound.

But as twilight draws near, the fights start to fade,
They gather together, this bond will not jade.
With heartwarming tales of their frosty careers,
They march homeward laughing, and ringing with cheers!

Frosty Fray

A snowy day, we gear up fast,
Laughter erupts, oh what a blast!
With chilly cheeks and wiggly toes,
We launch our flakes, the fun just grows.

Dodging left, I slip and slide,
A fluffy projectile hits my side!
In this frosty playground, we're all a mess,
Giggling loudly, we just want to press.

The snow spins wildly, a flurry so bright,
From the hilltop, we may take flight!
A snowman's head rolls past with glee,
"Is that aimed at me?" Oh, just wait and see!

With a final throw, we call it a truce,
Snowballs down, but laughter's let loose!
We'll remember this day, our frosty fray,
Till next time, friends, let's play away!

Hailstorm Havoc

The clouds roll in, oh what a sight,
A winter storm, it feels just right!
With friends in tow, we dash outside,
Time for a battle, the fun won't hide.

A hailstorm's coming, we'll have our fun,
But oh no, what's that? It's a hit-and-run!
Snowballs fly fast, sometimes in pairs,
One hit my brother, he's climbing up stairs!

With each new fling, our laughter swells,
The chaos around, it oddly compels.
A sudden flank from my sneaky mate,
Right to my face, can't seal my fate!

As twilight falls, we pelt the last round,
Snowflakes glimmer, all around.
A truce is declared, our ice-cold spree,
Tomorrow, my friend, let's do it with glee!

Powdered Vengeance

Whispers of snow, a plot to contrive,
Time for revenge, oh how we thrive!
I'll build up walls, a snowy defense,
Ready or not, for my powdered vengeance.

From behind a tree, I aim and take aim,
Launching my snowball, oh what a game!
Direct hit on my buddy, he's down for the count,
As laughter erupts, like snowflakes they mount.

My fortress stands tall, like a grand castle,
Yet chaos brews; this won't be a hassle!
Snowflies collide, it's a flurry of fun,
Each throw and splash, we're never outdone.

As the day fades, we gather around,
Crimson-faced friends, still snow-covered ground.
With powdered vengeance, our joy did arise,
Till next year, my pals, in this snowy surprise!

Icy Infraction

Gather 'round, it's that time of year,
Snowflakes fall and delight is near!
With gloves on tight, in the bright frosty morn,
We'll launch a barrage, our laughter reborn.

Slick icy patches lie in our way,
But we'll dodge them swiftly, it's all in the play!
With every sneak throw and every wild cheer,
We'll conquer the hills, spreading joy far and near.

When one takes a tumble, we all halt in surprise,
Head over heels, beneath snowy skies!
But up you get, and the fun resumes,
In this icy infraction, pure joy blooms.

As the sun starts to set, we pack up our fight,
Holding these memories, oh what a sight!
With giggles and joy, our hearts feel the glow,
Till next winter, my friends, for more icy show!

Whiteout Warfare

In the mounds of cold, we engage,
From behind a tree, like a sage.
A snowball whizzes past my ear,
Laughter erupts, it's time to cheer.

With madcap aim, I take my stance,
Launching missiles at every chance.
Each blow lands soft, yet sparks a laugh,
We're warriors here, on the snowy path.

A snow fort towering, walls of white,
We hurl our snowballs with delight,
Each hit a badge, a snowy scar,
Together we bliss, our frozen bazaar.

Then I trip on a hidden mound,
And with a thud, I'm face-to-ground.
Laughter erupts, my dignity fled,
In winter's hold, we'll forge ahead.

Sledding Saga

Down the hill, we race like fools,
With our sleds, defying the rules.
A tumble here, a slip and slide,
Snowy laughter, our winter pride.

Each belly flop, a joy to share,
In the crisp air, we haven't a care.
Twists and turns, and squeals of glee,
As we dash down, wild and free.

At the bottom, we crash in a pile,
Red noses and cheeks, mocks a smile.
More sleds queuing up for a ride,
In this wild winter, we take strides.

But wait, who's that, with a sneaky grin?
An avalanche starts, let the chaos begin!
We sail from the hill, like snow-crazed birds,
In sledding sagas, we lose our words.

Arctic Antics

In the fray, we frolic and flail,
Like penguins dancing without a trail.
Snowballs clashing, giggles abound,
In this winter wonder, fun is found.

With snow in our boots and ice on our nose,
Tripping over mounds as everyone goes.
A sneaky swipe, a clever attack,
With frosted cheeks, we won't hold back.

Snowmen army, all lined up tall,
We wage a war, will they stand or fall?
Each flurry a giggle, let's not get sore,
For in frozen realms, we always want more.

But oh, what's this? A grand snowball flies,
Straight for my face, oh how it dries!
In this act of antics, joy's our decree,
Together we laugh, both you and me.

Frostbite Fracas

Gather 'round for a frosty brawl,
In capes of white, we stand, so tall.
With snowflakes swirling in fray,
We come together for a winter play.

Whispers and giggles, plotting the strike,
Who will be hit, who will beike?
We pelt like ninjas, stealthy in snow,
Frostbite fracas, put on a show.

A snowball thrown, a dodge, a spin,
With each hit, grins widen, we all win.
We laugh through the chill, hearts in delight,
In this frosty tango, we dance through the night.

But oh, beware the snow's cruel grasp,
One wrong step and I find myself clasped.
Face full of snow, I'm hardly a threat,
Yet amidst frozen giggles, there's no regret.

Frosty Feuds

The snowflakes dance in the chilly air,
As warriors gather without a care.
With bundled coats and hats so bright,
They aim and fire, oh what a sight!

Laughter rings as a snowball flies,
Landing with a thud and a squeaky surprise.
A hidden foe with a crafty grin,
Launches a strike, let the games begin!

A soggy mitten, a slippery toe,
In the battle zone, the chaos will grow.
With giggles echoing, splatters abound,
Each icy splash a victory found!

But as the sun sets on this frosty spree,
The snowmen watch, amused as can be.
With cheeks all rosy and spirits so bright,
Who won the war? Oh, what a delight!

Snowy Siege

In a blanket of white, an army assembles,
With snow-packed ammo, the tension trembles.
A call to arms, the laughter erupts,
As snowballs launch, and the fun corrupts!

Behind the snow forts, they hide and they plot,
Strategic moves in a wintery lot.
But wait, oh no! A sneak attack!
Drenched and startled, there's no turning back!

With paths now muddied by flurry and cheer,
They dance through the drifts, no hint of fear.
A face full of snow, a bright snowfall crown,
The laughter ignites, and the tempers go down!

As twilight descends, they put down their might,
Regroup for hot cocoa, the end of the fight.
With marshmallows bobbing, a treaty so sweet,
In snowy tales, they find their retreat!

Chill Drifts

In the frosty dawn, the world is aglow,
Snow drifts piling up, oh what a show!
Giggles erupt as the kids storm outside,
With snowballs in hand, joy will not hide.

The wind it howls, the smiles they beam,
Behind towering forts, they plot, they scheme.
A snowy cannon, they load and prepare,
Fires of laughter, fill the brisk air!

A tumble, a slip, a snowball goes wide,
Lands on a head, oh how they all cried!
With cheeks that are rosy and spirits so high,
One hit blow, and the laughter can't die.

But as dusk falls, the fun doesn't cease,
They trade all their stories, shout, and release.
Amid the giggles, the chill, and the snow,
Memories made, proudly they all glow!

Hot Tempers

In the yard, a cold war erupts,
With laughter and shrieks, the chaos disrupts.
A flurry of snowballs, a sight to behold,
With stories of glory destined to be told.

Fingers go numb, cheeks rosy red,
Someone takes aim for a noggin instead.
The laughter grows loud while dodging a shot,
Each launch and retreat, a strategy sought!

A splash of wet snow brings tangled up cheer,
While clashes of snow draw friends ever near.
A little green sled becomes a trap door,
Launching a prank that ignites the uproar!

As shadows grow long, they shake off the chill,
With memories forged, their hearts surely thrill.
In the warmth of the house, as the fireplace glows,
They recount the battles, giggles still flow!

Blustery Battles

With wintery winds, the stage is set,
For boisterous battles, they'll never forget.
In layers of clothing, their cheeks all aglow,
They organize troops in the white-strewn show.

The first snowball flies and the fun takes flight,
Laughter surrounds thee with pure delight.
A strategic retreat, a stealthy disguise,
Snow slingshots fired, a pranking surprise!

Accidentally soaked, a shriek in the air,
As snowballs collide with whimsical flair.
With cheeks benumbed yet spirits so high,
In playful skirmishes, time seems to fly.

When the day fades, they gather around,
With mugs full of cocoa, sweet treats abound.
For every snow fight that fills them with glee,
Are stories eternal, just wait and see!

Frosty Foes

In the yard, we stock our stash,
Snowballs ready, hopes we'll clash.
Laughter echoes, cheeks aglow,
Here we go, it's time to throw!

Frothy flakes fly through the air,
Dodging snowballs with flair and care.
Each blizzard blast, a well-timed hit,
Who knew a snowball could be so lit!

Aiming for the crown, we wage our war,
But slippery ground leaves us on the floor.
Tumbles and giggles, it's pure delight,
Winning or losing, we're all silly sprites!

As the daylight fades, we call it a day,
Covered in snow, we laugh at our play.
With frozen fingers and rosy-red cheeks,
We'll remember this fun for all of the weeks!

Shiver and Sled

Sledding down the hill, what a thrill,
Upside down, we can't sit still.
Giggles and gasps, we race at break,
Into a drift, a snowy quake!

A snowball hits, it sharp and cold,
Smirks and glares, brave and bold.
A flurry of laughter, quick on our feet,
The chilly chase is such a treat!

Collecting snow, our weapons grow,
Aim for your friend, then duck low!
Flying projectiles, we're filled with glee,
Frosty combat, just you and me!

As the sun sets, our cheeks are bright,
Memories made in the frosty light.
An epic quest with laughter shared,
Shivering, sledding, not a moment spared!

Glacial Games

Gather 'round in winter flair,
Tossing snowballs without a care.
With icy clumps and a dash of wit,
We brave the cold for a frosty hit!

Slide and slip, roll into snow,
Surprise attack, here comes a show!
A sudden barrage, laughter erupts,
Chasing each other, so no one's upset!

Frozen opposition, we're bold and bright,
Tangled in snow, a glorious sight.
With giant drifts made to explore,
Snowmen rise, who could ask for more?

As darkness descends, the fun won't fade,
With a snack at the fire, our plans are laid.
Tomorrow again, we will vie for the crown,
In the glacial games, we won't back down!

Snow-Capped Fury

White peaks rise in sunset's glow,
A battlefield where all may go.
With laughter ringing, we chase and ski,
In our airy palace, wild and free!

With faces aglow from the frosty bite,
We stockpile snowballs with sheer delight.
Each throw, each dodge, our hearts all race,
A snow-capped fury in this frozen place!

"Look out!" I shout, as I throw a tree,
Oops, just a branch—was that a bee?
Chaos ensues, and everyone's fair,
Dancing through snow, our worries in air!

As stars twinkle above in winter's embrace,
We share tales of glory, each smile, each face.
With laughter and fun, we'll forever stay,
Chronicling joy in our own special way!

Frozen Fracas

In the frosty field, we gather near,
With frosty smiles and no hint of fear.
Snowballs packed tight, ready to throw,
The laughter erupts, with each flying snow.

Dodging and diving, a slippery dance,
Forget about aiming, it's all a chance!
A rogue snowball finds a face not intended,
The crowd bursts in giggles, all rules suspended.

Snowflakes tumble like giggling friends,
In this goofy battle, the fun never ends.
A hit on the hat, a splash on the coat,
Victory's sweet in this wintery moat.

As the snow settles, we shake off the cold,
With stories of triumph that never get old.
The epic remains of our powdery war,
Let's do it again! I simply adore!

Drifted Disputes

Beneath the blue sky, we plot our attack,
A brigade of snowballs, all ready to stack.
Launching with glee, we volley and laugh,
Who'll claim the crown in this silly behalf?

Aiming for friends like it's all in good fun,
But misfires fly, hitting Dad—uh-oh, run!
He shakes off the snow with a grumpy old glare,
Yet can't help but chuckle, caught unaware.

The bushes are hiding the biggest of foes,
With all of our ammo, we strike deadly blows.
But wait, what's this? A snowball brigade,
A counterattack is incredibly made!

As curtains fall on this lively affair,
With cold noses red and snow in our hair.
With hot cocoa warming our giggling tummies,
Those drifted disputes shall turn into memories.

White-Washed Warfare

Our army is small, but our aim is quite grand,
With mittened hands we take our icy stand.
Laughter ensues as snowballs take flight,
In this white-washed war, we jest through the night.

Whispers of strategy, mud pies in disguise,
A blizzard of laughter as cold drops surprise.
Flakes turn to missiles in our carefree mirth,
Exploding in giggles, a battle of worth.

Old man Jenkins yells from his creaky old chair,
But he's just a target for snow to ensnare.
His glasses slapped clean with a snowy delight,
He joins in our frolic, hearts soaring in flight.

With clumps on our heads and our cheeks all aglow,
We march off with joy, our spirits in tow.
This white-washed warfare, an epic before,
May the laughter continue forevermore!

Cold Confrontation

With jackets on tight, we engage in the fight,
At the edge of the park, laughter fills up the night.
Snowballs are flying, a flurry of cheer,
In this cold confrontation, nothing to fear!

Sneaky ambushes from behind the tall trees,
We dodge and we dart like the swift little bees.
A plop on my hat sends me right into glee,
I'm plotting revenge—just you wait and see!

The snow is our canvas, the laughter our paint,
With splashes of joy, no room for complaint.
A throw goes awry, it's a slippery game,
Yet how could we falter? It's all just the same!

As the daylight wanes and our energy fades,
The war effort simmers, we're all just cascades.
We share all our tales by the warm fireplace,
In this cold confrontation, we found our own place.